DIDDLY DOODLES

Winnie
-the-
Pooh

A. A. Milne with decorations by Andy Grey

DEAN

Diddly Doodles Winnie-the-Pooh
first published in Great Britain 2018
by Dean, an imprint of Egmont UK Limited,
The Yellow Building, 1 Nicholas Road, London W11 4AN.

©2018 Disney Enterprises, Inc
Based on the "Winnie-the-Pooh" works by A. A. Milne and E. H. Shepard
Illustrations by Andrew Grey

ISBN 978
703
Printed in

D1332845

Stay safe online. Egmont is not responsible for content hosted by third parties.

Egmont takes its responsibility to the planet and its inhabitants very seriously.
We aim to use papers from well-managed forests run by responsible suppliers.

Meet the Characters

Kanga

Winnie-the-Pooh

Owl

Piglet

Roo

Christopher
Robin

Eeyore

Rabbit

Tigger

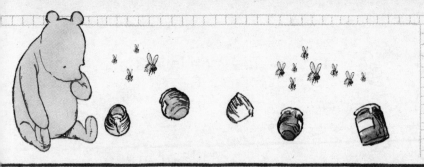

TO NORTH POLE

BIG STONES
AND ROX

BEE
TREE

RABBITS FrENDS
AND RALEtIONS

MY
HOUSE

OWLS
HOUSE

100 AKER
WOOD

EEYORES
GLOOMY PLACE

RATHER BOGGY
AND SAD

Winnie-the-Pooh loves honey.

Draw some bees buzzing around his head.

Pooh is floating away.

Give Tigger, Rabbit and Piglet
balloons, too, so they can join him.

It's raining in the Hundred Acre Wood.

What colour is Christopher Robin's umbrella?

Eeyore has lost his tail.

Can you draw him a new one?

Christopher Robin and Pooh are
best friends.

Colour in this picture
of the friends together.

Tigger is looking at himself in the mirror –
draw his reflection!

It's a fine day for
hunting Woozles
and Pooh is on
their trail.

Draw who has joined him!

Kanga is hunting high and low for somebody.

Kanga

Rabbit

Piglet

Roo

Follow the wiggly lines with your finger
to find out who Kanga is looking for.

Roo

Here's a

Poem about Eeyore

Eeyore is old, he's grey and he's slow,
He may, if you're lucky, nod a hello,
But he's probably pondering a sad reflection
And thinking with gloom of his sorry dejection.

Eeyore eats thistles, and wonders "Why?"
He may, if you're lucky, look up with a sigh,
But mostly his low expectations are such
That he's grateful to any who think of him much.

Decorate the poem!

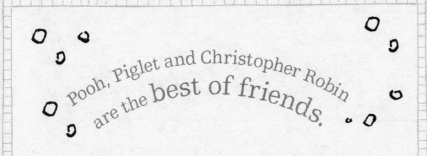

Pooh, Piglet and Christopher Robin are the best of friends.

Colour them in!

Christopher Robin is reading
Pooh a story

and what a lovely story
it will be.

Roo and Tigger are throwing fir-cones
to one another.

Draw the fir-cones
flying around in the wind!

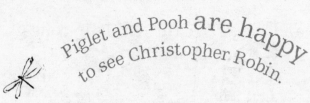

Piglet and Pooh are happy
to see Christopher Robin.

Colour him in a smart raincoat and hat!

Colour in
Tigger

as he
bounces high

and low.

Hooray

it's a picnic!

Draw what Christopher Robin
is showing Pooh and Piglet.

Pooh needs all
of his friends to
help when he
is stuck!

Draw some more if you think he needs them.

Piglet is stranded!
Draw in the rain that is causing the flood!

Pooh, Piglet and Christopher Robin
are floating in an umbrella.

What colour should it be?

What a mess!

Pooh, Piglet and Owl have taken
a tumble.

What is Christopher Robin
daydreaming about?

Pooh is doing his stoutness exercises.

Draw his reflection!

Pooh and his friends have found
a rainbow.

Colour it in with bright colours!

Pooh has unwrapped
a present.

Draw what you think it is!

Here's a

Poem about Piglet

Piglet is Small
But that's not all:
His bravery shows
That when the wind blows
His dear friends mean more than ever before
As he battles his way through a bluster.

? So what does he do? ?
With persuasion from Pooh,
He climbs up some string
(What a Very Grand Thing),
To go and fetch help (not so much as a yelp)
And save his dear friends from a fluster.

Decorate the poem!

Poor Piglet's present to Eeyore has popped.

Draw in a big bang!

Someone has poked their head into Rabbit's house.

Draw who you think it is!

What a fun lunch!

Draw some delicious food for Pooh
and his friends to enjoy.

Piglet is
thinking about
a story Pooh
just told him.

Draw what you think it was about.

Owl has found his favourite picture.

What do you think it shows?

What has
Kanga got in
her pouch?

Here's a

Poem about Christopher Robin

He's a boy who cares
About Piglets and Bears,
About picnics and teas
And rescues from trees –
Hip-hip for skipping and hopping!

He's a boy who smiles
At the silliest wiles,
At the funniest cares
Of Piglets and Bears –

Hooray for Christopher Robin!

Decorate the poem!

Pooh, Christopher Robin and Piglet are having a lovely time by the stream.

Colour in this picture
of the friends together.

What's floating by?

Tigger and Pooh are
tucking into some honey.

Make the honey yellow and bright!

Piglet has bought
Tigger a present.

Draw what's in the basket.

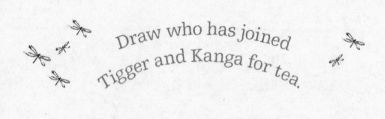

Draw who has joined
Tigger and Kanga for tea.

What a fun game!

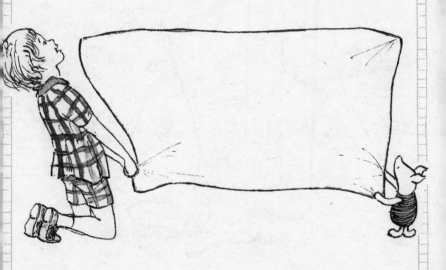

What colour is the blanket that
Christopher Robin and Piglet are
using to bounce Tigger?

Pooh is about to play a
game of Poohsticks.

Draw some friends
to play with him.

Eeyore must be ever so cold.

Draw the snow on his back.

Pooh and his friends have spotted
something in the river. What is it?

Eeyore is floating in the river.

Draw some ducks to keep him company.

Rabbit is hungry. Draw some food for him to eat.

Pooh is searching for something in his cupboard.

Draw something for him to find.

Piglet is tucked up in bed.

Colour him a bright and cosy bedspread.

Who has knocked on Piglet's door?

What have Christopher Robin and Piglet found hiding in a hole in the Hundred Acre Wood?

What is Piglet *running* away from?

Is it a Woozle? Or a Heffalump?

Christopher Robin and Pooh
are having a lovely walk in
the Hundred Acre Wood.

Draw some flowers for them to smell!

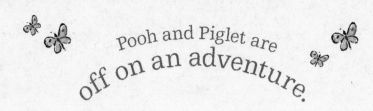

Pooh and Piglet are
off on an adventure.

Draw where they are heading off to.

Pooh has spotted something in the sky.
Draw what you think it is!

Here's a

Poem about Tigger

He came to the Forest late one night,
The noise was enough to give Pooh a fright.
"Worraworraworra," he said,
And Pooh got out of bed,
To find a Bouncy Tigger ahead.

Tigger now lives with Kanga and Roo,
Eating enough Medicine for two!
Never was an animal bouncier than he,
(Except when he was stuck up a tree.)

A Friendlier Tigger there never will be!

Decorate the poem!

It's a sunny day in
the Hundred Acre Wood.

Draw Pooh a hat
to keep him in the shade!

Owl is having a nice snooze in a tree.

Draw some birds
flying around his head –
hopefully their tweets won't wake him up!

Pooh is having a lovely walk,
looking at the sky.

Draw some clouds
in funny shapes.

Winnie-the-Pooh
is a yellow bear.

Colour him in!

Owl is hiding under a blanket.

What colour is it?

Tigger is looking at a butterfly.

Draw some more for him to enjoy!

Pooh and his friends have
made a snowman.

Draw some eyes, arms, buttons and
a hat to keep him warm.

Draw a big pile of
honey pots behind Pooh!

Kanga and Piglet are bouncing fast.

Draw some friends running
along with them!

It's cosy by the fire.

Colour in some bright patterns
for the wallpaper and the armchair.

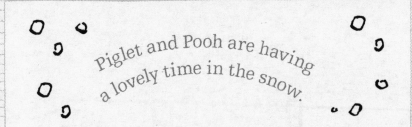

Piglet and Pooh are having a lovely time in the snow.

Draw a snowman for them to play with.

What's Tigger looking at?

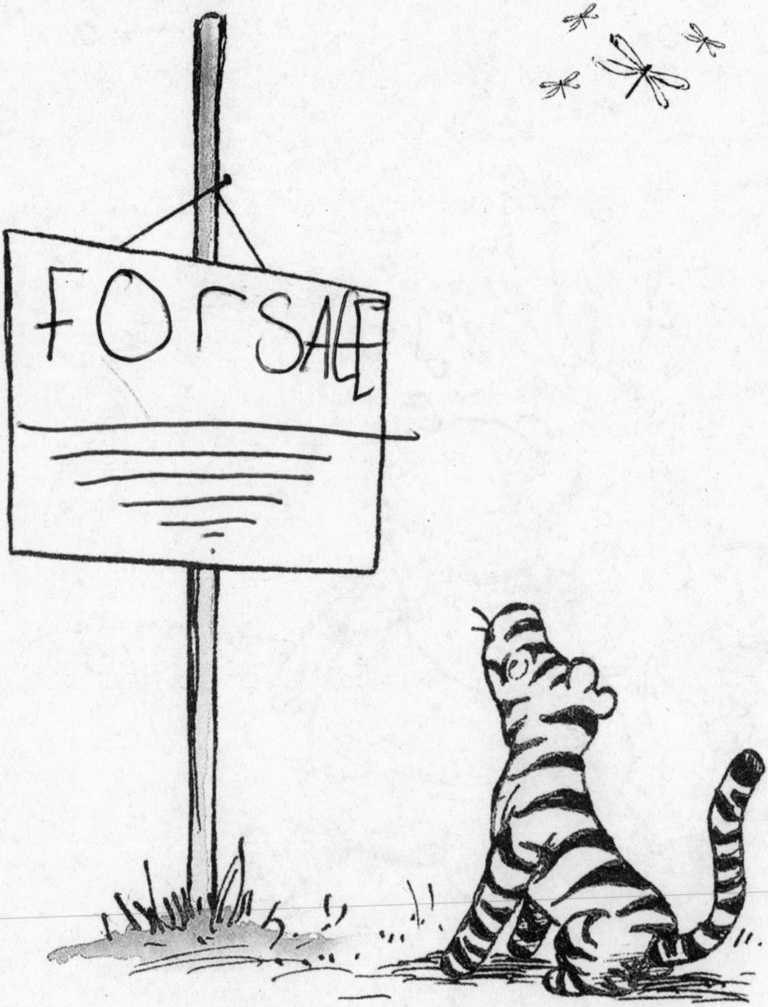

Eeyore looks sad today.

Draw something to make him happy!

Eeyore is alone by the stream.
Draw some friends to keep him company.

What has Pooh spotted on the floor?

Pooh has thrown a stone in the river.

Draw a big SPLASH!

Christopher Robin, Pooh and Piglet have spotted something interesting.

What do you think it is?

Here's a

Poem about Pooh

Pooh is a Silly Old Bear
Who lives life without a care.
He's happiest when he has honey,
The taste of it makes him go funny,
Goloptious honey, sticky and runny!

That clever Bear of Little Brain,
Saved Piglet from the pouring rain!
There's nothing that he wouldn't do,
Life is fun with friends like you.

The Best Bear in All the World – Pooh!

Decorate the poem!

What colour is the front door Piglet is trying to knock?

Owl and Pooh are painting a pot for Eeyore's birthday.

Cover it in bright patterns.

Tigger has lost his stripes –
draw them back in!

It's a very windy day.
Draw some leaves in
different shapes.

Owl is flying home
for tea with Pooh.

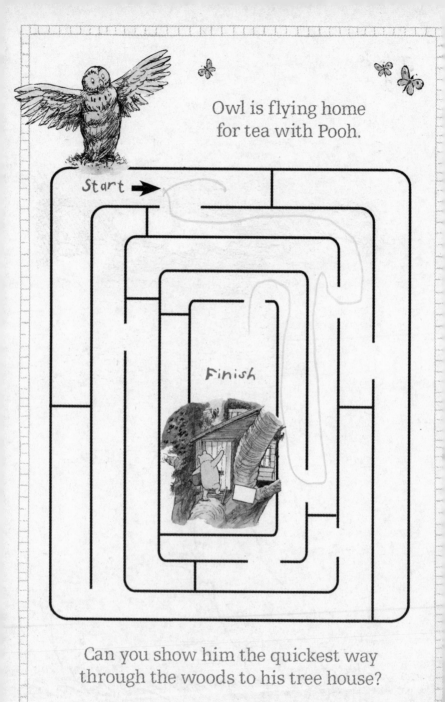

Start ➤

Finish

Can you show him the quickest way
through the woods to his tree house?

It's Eeyore's house

Draw some visitors for him!

Goodnight
Winnie-the-Pooh!

Draw his dream.